THE GREAT BOOK OF ANIMAL KNOWLEDGE

KOALAS

Furry Marsupials of Australia

Introduction

Koalas are furry mammals that can be found in Australia. Although many people call them "koala bears", koalas are not bears, they are tree climbing, leaf-eating marsupials.

What Koalas Look Like

When Europeans first saw koalas, they thought it was some kind of bear or monkey. Although koalas aren't related to bears or monkeys, they look like small teddy bears. Koalas have large furry ears, small black eyes, and a large nose.

Size and Weight

Koalas grow 2 to almost 3 feet tall, and they can weigh up to 20 pounds. Southern koalas are bigger and almost 2 times heavier than northern koalas. Most males are also bigger and heavier than females.

Fur

A koala's fur is colored grey or brown. Their fur is thick and fluffy to protect them from both high and low temperatures. Their thick fur also acts as a raincoat during rainy days.

Paws

The paws of koalas are designed for climbing trees. Two fingers on their front paws are separated from the other three, like our thumbs, to make holding branches easier. They also have sharp claws and pads on their paws that help them in climbing.

Sounds

Photo by Andy Hay (flickr.com/andyhay), as licensed under CC BY 2.0 Generic

The sound male koalas make surprises some people. They make a deep 'belching' sound. It also sounds like a very deep roar. Koalas can also make some other sounds like shrieking.

Where Koalas Live

Photo by LilyRose97 (flickr.com/11747587@N08), as licensed under CC BY 2.0 Generic

Koalas can be found in the eastern parts of Australia. They live in the tree tops of eucalyptus forests. Each koala has their own tree where they live.

What Koalas Eat

Photo by Travis (flickr.com/travoc), as licensed under CC BY 2.0 Generic

Koalas are herbivores, which means they don't eat meat. The favorite food of a koala is the leaves from eucalyptus trees. Eucalyptus leaves are actually poisonous to other animals, but koalas have bacteria in their stomach that break down the toxic oils. Koalas are picky about which eucalyptus leaves they eat, there are lots of species of eucalyptus but they only eat a few kinds.

Senses

Photo by cyrusbulsara (flickr.com/cyrusbulsara), as licensed under CC BY 2.0 Generic

Koalas have a very good sense of smell. Their other senses, seeing and hearing, aren't quite as good as their sense of smell. Koalas use their strong sense of smell to pick only the best leaves to eat. Their sense of smell also helps them find eucalyptus trees from far away.

Drinking

Photo by Aaron Jacobs (flickr.com/aaronjacobs), as licensed under CC BY-SA 2.0 Generic

Koalas will drink if water is available. However, they actually don't really need to drink as much as other animals. They get most of their moisture from the leaves they eat. In fact, the word 'Koala' means 'no water'!

What Koalas Do

Photo by Better Than Bacon (flickr.com/slurm), as licensed under CC BY 2.0 Generic

Koalas are usually awake during the night and asleep during the day. Because their diet of eucalyptus leaves is fibrous and contains little nutrition, koalas have to sleep a lot every day to save energy. They spend 18-20 hours a day sleeping! When awake, they spend most of their time eating.

Territory

Each koala has their own home range. These home ranges contain several home trees that the koala visits regularly. The home ranges of koalas overlap with each other sometimes. Koalas mark their territory by leaving scratch marks on their trees. Males also have a dark scent gland on their chests. They rub their chest on trees to leave a scent marking.

Fighting Each Other

An alpha male's home range covers several female's home ranges. To protect his home range the alpha male will have to fight off other males that want to take over his home range. Koalas don't always fight, and when they do, they don't usually get injured. Koalas fight by pushing and biting each other.

Breeding

Photo by JoyTek (flickr.com/joytek), as licensed under CC BY-SA 2.0 Generic

Koalas mate anytime from August to February. They usually give birth to one baby koala (called a joey) each breeding season, but sometimes they give birth to twins. Female koalas are pregnant for around 35 days before giving birth.

Pouches

Photo by Kim (flickr.com/thegirlsny), as licensed under CC BY-SA 2.0 Generic

Female koalas, like all other animals in the marsupial family, have pouches. The pouch of a koala is open downward, but the baby koala won't fall off because the mother uses strong muscles to keep it closed. Mother koalas carry their babies in their pouch until the babies are too big to fit inside.

Baby Koalas

Photo by belgianchocolate (flickr.com/frank-wouters), as licensed under CC BY 2.0 Generic

Koalas are born blind, furless, and completely helpless. They are so small, they only measure around 1 inch! Newborn koalas stay in their mother's pouch drinking milk. Eucalyptus leaves are still poisonous for baby koalas. When they reach about 7 months old their mother gives them special droppings called 'pap' so they can start eating the eucalyptus leaves.

Life of a Koala

Baby koalas live in their mother's pouch for about six months. After this they ride on their mother's back or belly. They still return to the pouch once in a while to drink milk until they are too big to fit inside. Koalas leave their mother when she has another joey, this usually happens when they are 1-3 years old. When koalas leave their mothers they have to find their own territory.

Predators

Koalas don't have very many predators. Eagles and owls sometimes hunt koalas, and other big predator birds hunt young koalas. Dingoes and sometimes domestic dogs will also kill koalas if they are caught on the ground.

Endangered

Photo by Frankzed (flickr.com/frankzed), as licensed under CC BY 2.0 Generic

During the early 1900s millions of koalas were killed by hunting. Today, koalas are a protected species, which means that they are not allowed to be hunted. However koalas have a new problem. The eucalyptus forests where they live are being cut at a fast rate. Koalas rely on the eucalyptus forests for their home and for their food. Without it they will not survive. Many koalas also die by getting hit by automobiles.

Relatives

Koalas are part of the marsupial family. Marsupials are a class of mammals living primarily in Australia and the Americas. Most marsupials carry their young in pouches. Other marsupials include kangaroos, opossums, wombats and wallabies. Wombats are koalas' closest relatives.

Subspecies

Photo by Therea digitalkiwi (flickr.com/digitalkiwi), as licensed under CC BY-SA 2.0 Generic

There are 3 commonly recognized subspecies of koala. These are the Queensland, Victorian and New South Wales koalas. Each species differs in fur color and thickness, body size, and skull shape. Queensland koalas are the smallest of the 3, and they have short silver fur. Victorian koalas are the largest, they have thick brown fur.

Get the next book in this series!

CAMELS: Ships of the Desert

Log on to Facebook.com/GazelleCB for more info

Tip: Use the key-phrase "The Great Book of Animal Knowledge" when searching for books in this series.

For more information about our books, discounts and updates, please Like us on FaceBook!

Facebook.com/GazelleCB

41518294R00015

Made in the USA
Columbia, SC
14 December 2018